Find Your Purpose.

Manage Your Career.

By Aaron Basko

Contents

Introduction

"The purpose of life is a life of purpose." —
Robert Byrne

Imagine yourself in a fancy ballroom. It is full of well-dressed people coming and going, and networking with each other. As people walk by, you notice that they are wearing name tags, the kind that say, "Hello my name is… ." But as you look at each one, you notice that they are not traditional names.

Instead, they are things like "Customer Service Rock Star," "One Woman Welcoming Committee," "Makes Others Feel Safe," "The Idea Guy," "Never Met a Stranger," "I Make Everything More Fun," or a "Fearless inventor."

After a while, you realize that these are not just names; they actually have captured the essence of what these people do. That makes you wonder, when you look down at your own name tag, what will you see?

Take a moment to think about this. If you had to write a name like this for yourself, what would it be?

Most of us spend the majority of our lives looking for the name on our name tag. But for too many people it is not an intentional search. Instead, we go through life wondering why we don't fit into a simple job description or why our interests don't seem to be enough to satisfy us.

This book is about discovering the name that belongs on your name tag. It's about finding out who you really are and what you were born to do. When you know that, you are able to move forward confidently in your life and make better decisions. Best of all, this knowledge gives you a tool that allows you to manage your career for a lifetime.

Decades ago, people trained for one career where they would spend their entire working lives, sometimes even at just one company. Those days are long gone, however, and now most people will make many career decisions in a lifetime. What do we base them on? What field is hot? Where can you make more money? How will you know if you are making the right choice?

By discovering your purpose, you discover a ruler by which you can measure every career choice you need to make. Use this book to discover your unique design and how you can use it to do what you are told to do.

I describe my way of helping people find their purpose as the "Three Keys Method." These three keys are "Design," "Desire," and "Demand." Successfully balancing these elements will help you create a deep sense of purpose that guides you in your career choices and career development. We will look at each of these three keys in the following chapters to give you a better understanding of how to develop them and use them to maximize your potential. It is the overlap of these elements that pinpoints your purpose and feeds your success. As we go along, I will show you exercises you can use to better define these keys in your own life. And we will put them all together to look at how you can begin managing your career today.

CHAPTER 1:

Discovering Your Design

"The purpose of life is not to be happy. It is to be useful, to be honorable, to be compassionate, to have it make some difference that you have lived and lived well." — Ralph Waldo Emerson

I'm a person of faith. I have a deep belief that people were created by God as unique individuals. I see

them as handcrafted tools to accomplish a purpose. Why do I believe this?

Partly, it is from my own experience with God, and the ways I believe I've seen Him work directly in my life. I've been fortunate to always have had a sense of His presence, and to maintain an ongoing conversation with Him about my daily life. To me, He is a "person," not the "thing" that is up there somewhere.

But beyond my personal experience, I also looked at the world and I listened to my simple logic. Nothing that you see around you is purposeless. No matter where you look, everything serves its function.

Whether we look at the seasons, the weather, the ecosystem, the food chain, or whatever other natural phenomenon we choose, there is order and there is meaning.

The same is true with people. Everything we create has its own function. If you bake a cake, it is to appease hunger or celebrate a birthday. If it is a piece of music, it tries to delight or teach or encourage others to feel something. Even if you're inventing a wraparound couch, it is to provide comfort, relaxation, and a good view of the football game on TV.

If everything we see in the world has a function — a purpose and job to fulfill — it only stands to reason that we do as well. Humans have a purpose in the world, but more specifically, YOU have a purpose in the world.

TOOLS IN THE TOOLBOX

Finding your purpose starts with discovering your design. Let me share an analogy.

A builder who wants to build a house takes a variety of tools with him to do the job. Each tool has its specific function. Part of what separates the builder from everyone else is that he knows which tool to employ and when. I think this is how God uses people in the world as well. He made some people to act as hammers, some people are screwdrivers, some people saws, some people wrenches, etc. He then invites us into interesting places in the world to apply our specific function to make an impact.

Can you paint a wall with a hammer? Or drive a nail with a paintbrush? Sure, theoretically you can. But it will cause you a lot of frustration and create a huge mess. If you are a hammer, you need to be clear that your job is to pound nails. If you are a paintbrush, you need to understand that you are meant for painting walls. So many people go through life wishing to be a different kind of tool than the one that they are. They end up becoming less successful and more stressed than they need to be. If they were able to discover their design and had the courage to follow it, they would find a life that is more meaningful and gives them greater impact.

WHAT IS DESIGN?

Your design is your gift. It is what you are created to do and what you tend to do very naturally, more so than other people around you. When you use your design, you have an outsized impact on the world.

Often this will surprise others, who will compliment you for your skills in this area, although you feel like it is something everyone should be able to do.

Think about it like this: Design answers the question, "Who am I and what am I meant to do?"

Your design has a certain determination about it. It does not like to be put off or ignored. If we pick careers for jobs that don't fit well with our design, it haunts us. We are restless, unsatisfied, and have this nagging feeling that we were meant for something else. When we achieve things without it, we tend to feel empty and lost. Sometimes our design is pursuing us as much as we are pursuing it. It leaves us amazing clues throughout our lives because it wants to be discovered. So, how do we find it?

One of the coolest ways to search for evidence of your design is to take a look in the rearview mirror. Did you ever notice that many kids develop strong personality traits early on, which later get balanced out in their lives? While we often see these as behavioral issues, I think in many cases it is a child working from his or her design but not yet doing it very well. It is like that particular skill develops first, before the other things that would make for a well-rounded person. Because of this, childhood is often a great place to look for clues about someone's design.

Think of the people that you know and the funny things that you remember about them when they were younger. What does it tell you about them now?

Some kids start putting bandages on their stuffed animals at the age of four. They grow up to be people who work in helping professions with a strong sense of empathy for other people.

One of my friends, the class clown, networks in entertainment in Hollywood.

One of my nephew's kindergarten teachers nicknamed him "The Mayor" because of his love of checking in on everyone and assigning them things to do.

I was one of those kinds of kids too, whose design was hard to contain. My one "C" in conduct was in

second grade. When my parents went to the parent-teacher conference, they were told that I was a good kid, but that I finished my work and then went around distracting everyone by trying to help them with theirs. All these years later, not much has changed!

As you think about your design, what clues come from your childhood? Talk with your parents, or with someone else who knew you well when you were young. What kinds of things did you get in trouble for? What did people notice that was different about you from other kids? Can you see how that relates to who you are now? Are you still trying to use the same skills? Take a minute and write down where you think your design might have peeked its head out when you were younger:

My Purpose

My design has always been connected with helping people achieve their potential. I love to really "see" people, to understand them, and help them see and understand themselves. I love to make people feel special, and I do it as a way of empowering them and motivating them to take the steps to move forward in their lives so that they can be who they were meant to be.

Again, I connect this to my faith. There is a verse in the Bible that says:

"My purpose is that they may be encouraged in heart and united in love, so that they may have the full

riches of complete understanding, in order that they may know the mystery of God, namely Christ."
— Colossians 2:2

This verse has always made a lot of sense to me. I see myself encouraging people and trying to bring them together so that they will see themselves more clearly and be able to achieve more. I have written this out into a personal purpose statement for myself:

"To help others see who they are and imagine who they could become."

This is the yardstick that I use in evaluating all the work that I do. Whether writing a book, making a presentation, meeting with someone for coaching, or building and developing a team, my goal is always to help people see themselves more clearly and to catch a vision of their own future if they could maximize their gifts.

Having this purpose statement is incredibly helpful in my decision-making process. When an opportunity comes along, I can ask myself, "Is this in line with my purpose statement, or is it a distraction from it?"

I'm certainly not the only person to live from this kind of purpose statement. I look at history and I see people who have risen to incredible success because they understood their design. That sense of purpose is what separates the great presidents of the United States — the ones we remember — from those who are largely forgettable. It is evident in the lives of civil rights leaders, technology geniuses, and people of great faith. It is good practice to think about famous leaders and try to put into words what purpose they might have been trying to live out.

We were created to fulfill a purpose, and doing so is where we get our power and effectiveness for living.

THE THREE MOVIES EXERCISE

One of my favorite activities to guide people through is one called the "Three Movies Exercise." It is fun because it is something that almost everyone can relate to, and it shows how deeply we recognize the importance of purpose at an unconscious level. It goes like this:

Sit for a minute and think of your three or four favorite movies. Take your time to think of the ones that have resonated consistently with you.

Now take a few minutes and try to summarize the basic plot line of these movies in just a few sentences.

Let me share my example:

My favorite movies are the original *Matrix* movie, the *Lord of the Rings* trilogy ("That still only counts as one!" for those of you who are fans), and *The Last Samurai*. What do all of these movies have in common, besides swords? In each movie, there is a protagonist who does not believe he is a hero. He meets a mentor character who believes in him and trains him. Then the hero then goes out and saves the world.

I know it sounds strange, but if you look at each of these movies, they follow that same basic narrative. That tells me that something in that narrative resonates deeply with me.

Now here's the really interesting part. Look at the list of movies that you came up with and their story lines and pick out which character you most identify with.

For example, in my case, it is not actually the hero with whom I identify the most. It is actually the mentor character. In *The Matrix* it is Morpheus. In *Lord of the Rings* it is Gandalf. In *The Last Samurai* it is Katsumoto. In each of these cases, I relate to the character who comes alongside the hero, encourages him and helps him to reach his full potential, instilling in him the confidence that he needs to take on the world. That sounds suspiciously like my purpose statement, doesn't it?

Most people find that when they analyze the movies that move them the most, they see in their favorite character a design that they long for. Try it out and see if it is not true for you.

We love and identify with these stories because they tell us something deep about ourselves. They point to us who we really are, and who we were meant to be. So, use all of your resources, whether they are movies, books, stories, or the tales about you when you were a little kid. They're all clues, like the fingerprints of God on your life.

CHAPTER 2:

Assessing Your Design

"We all have a purpose in life, and when you find yours you will recognize it." — *Catherine Pulsifer*

If you've followed me so far, the questions you should be asking are, "Okay, so what tool am I?" This is where the next assessment comes in. This chapter is a question-based exploration intended to help you discover or clarify your design. To figure out what your design is, it can be helpful to look for clues to the function you have, and probably already have been using, but may not recognize.

Assessment Instructions

This quiz is a subjective assessment, with no right or wrong answers. It is not intended to give you an exact match with a specific job title, but to help you to pinpoint your special function. To take the assessment you should:

1. Answer each question thoughtfully, with as much detail as possible, preferably written down. After each answer, ask whether you have answered the "Why?" question. Why did

I choose this response? Why do I prefer this choice?

2. Ask two other people you trust to answer these same questions about you. Ideally, one would be a parent or family member who has known you well since you were very young. The other could be a friend who knows you well now. Compare their answers with your answers to find themes or to consider some things you do very naturally and don't consider that special. Often others will see them as very special indeed.

3. Use the follow-up instructions after the assessment for help in identifying themes and creating a purpose statement.

4. Over the next few weeks, think about what you have learned. Get feedback from others about whether what you have come up with accurately reflects who you are and what you do.

5. Apply it to your choices. Learn all you can about the careers and roles that will best allow you to use this purpose (more about this below).

DESIGN ASSESSMENT

1. List three high points in your life and the reason why they qualify. These should be moments when you really felt you were "on" or were using your gifts, but they don't have to be huge accomplishments.

2. Name one or two highlights that you have experienced in the last week?

3. Why do your friends seek you out for help? Do they come to you for acceptance? Is it because they can count on you? If they were asked what your best qualities are, what would they say?

4. Name a job or class that you really did not enjoy. Be as specific as possible about why it was not a good match. Did it bother you to deal with people's problems all day? If it was a class, was it too theoretical, too structured? Give examples.

5. What role do you play in your family (or did you play growing up)? Did you take care of siblings? Are you the peacemaker? Are you the one who loves to plan family adventures?

6. What one thing that you do would gain your enemy's respect? For example, if someone did not like you, they might say, "Well, he or she drives me crazy, but at least....he is hones, she fights for what she believes in, he plays good guitar, etc."

7. If you could be internationally recognized for doing one good thing, what would it be?

8. What do people thank you for?

9. Would you rather work with people, ideas (writing, research, experimenting), or objects (machines, building, etc.)?

10. What personality traits did your parents pass on to you that you like in yourself?

11. What minor things did you get in trouble for when you were younger?

FINDING YOUR THEMES

Once you have written out the answers to your assessment, and hopefully given it out to a couple of people who know you well, it is time to look for clues. What are the threads that run through your answers that will help you get a clearer sense of your purpose?

1. Start with question 9. People usually have a clear initial reaction and find this easy to answer. The key here is that your two first choices will typically work in some combination in your purpose, with your first choice leading. Just as important, you can probably clear a large number of jobs and roles off the table by eliminating things related to choice three. For example, my first two choices are people

and ideas. Objects are a clear third choice. That means I can pretty confidently eliminate jobs or roles that involve hands-on manipulation of objects (construction, repair, many areas of hands-on-science, much manufacturing and assembly, areas or engineering, managing supplies, etc.)

It is a good confirmation that when you hear these types of jobs, they don't stir any interest. If your third choice is people, you can probably eliminate areas of customer service, counseling, teaching, nursing, sales, hospitality, ministry, human services, etc.

If your third area is ideas, steer clear of research, writing, higher education leadership, and most areas of traditional science. Think for a minute about what you can safely eliminate.

2. Now let's look at a second category of questions, 10 and 11. Sometimes your design shows clearly very early in life. Some people's purpose may be to care for others in some area of health or wellness began by bandaging stuffed animals at an early age. Others were constantly inventing unconventional solutions, memorizing everything they saw, or creating harmony between people in conflict. Getting some feedback about what traits you have always had can be helpful. Looking for family traits can also help. If there are some things you like about yourself that were clearly passed on, they may be clues.

3. Now think about some of those important moments that have helped to teach you who you are. Your answer to question 1 is an essential one. What are you looking for is a theme or themes among the moments you identify as best. Why did you feel so "on" at these moments? What were you actually doing? If you had to describe what kind of tool you were then, what would you say? Is there a connection between your different answers? When you consider question 2, are you using any of those same types of skills on a daily basis and enjoying them? Where do you get day to day?

4. Conversely, check your answer for #4. What does it say about what drains your energy? Does this seem like the opposite of what you found in #1 and #2? Does it fit into the area you chose last in #9?

5. What themes do you notice about what energizes and inspires you?

6. Think about your life now. Read your answers to #3, #5, #6, and #8. How do others perceive you and what do they think you do best/ Sometimes your gifts – making others feel comfortable, speaking persuasively, inspiring confidence, breaking problems into logical steps, providing a listening ear – seem so natural to you that they don't stand out. Knowing how you affect others when you do what you do best can reveal a lot about what you should be doing.

7. Finally, think about the future with question 7. If you had no concerns about making money or titles, or what other would think about your work, what would you want to do on a daily basis? Which of your skills and talents could you use daily and feel energized, rather than drained? What would you most want to be remembered for doing? At the end of your life, you would want to describe yourself as someone who always…did what? (For example, looked out for those in need, helped others understand each other better, discovered truths that improved out knowledge of the world, etc.)

DESIGN STATEMENT

Taking the information you have written above, begin forming your answers into patterns. Where do you see things that match? Maybe you see several questions that indicate you like to discover things – solutions, the answers to puzzles, what happens when you combine chemicals. Maybe you find that you are always taking care of people and helping them feel better. Or maybe you are the person others come to for expertise when they need something put together correctly. Do these things bring you joy? How can you put them into an action sentence?

Starting with the word "to," begin making the theme you picked out into a phrase that best describes what you do well and love doing. Here are some examples:

- To use care and compassion to help hurting people feel better
  To build things with excellence that people will marvel at

- To uncover secrets in the world around us

- To bring order into the environments where I live and work

- To listen and give wise counsel that will improve people's lives

- To help people recognize unfairness and injustice and inspire them to change it To help others see and reach their potential

- To use technology to solve people's problems

It may take time for something to resonate with you. Keep trying out your possibilities until something really calls to you. If you have possibilities, write them out here:

TEST IT OUT

Thinking of design in this way is a huge help in correctly evaluating complex career decisions. Too often money, benefits, title, or organization sway our decisions. So, we choose what we think we "should" do, rather than what we were made to do. If, on the other hand, you know your design, you can use it to make wise decisions — knowing that the more time you spend fulfilling your function, the more effective you will be.

CHAPTER 3:

Discovering Your Desire

"If you don't feel it, flee from it. Go where you are celebrated, not merely tolerated." - Paul F. Davis

The second of the three keys is your desire. This is obviously not the desire of romance novels, but what is that deep longing to learn, to explore, to understand, and to give back. Many people confuse design with desire, or think they're the same thing. If you understand them, they support one another and help you to be effective in making an impact on the world, but they are two different things.

Design answers the "what" question: "What should I do with my life? What skills should I be using?"

Desire answers a different question, which we could phrase as, "Where should I be doing it, or for whom should I be doing it?"

Desire is typically much easier to discover. It is closer to our consciousness of ourselves. We express it much more often. When we're career-searching, we often will say things like, "I think I would like to work in medicine, or education, or the arts." We have areas of knowledge that attract us, and we have different types of people we're drawn to and we like to interact with. These are our desires at work.

The word desire is a dangerous one to use because it has many connotations. Oftentimes people shy away from it, not just because of its romantic significance, but because it seems to imply something very selfish. I would say that it is not so much selfish as it is personal. We don't have a lot of control over design; that is how we are made. But desire is what we bring to the table. It is our collective set of interests, positive experiences, and visions for our future selves.

This set of attributes can be very inspiring, and can motivate people to great accomplishments for the betterment of the world. If they want to use our analogy from the previous chapter, some hammers build houses and some build birdhouses. Some are specially equipped for framing, while others are used for gently tapping. Our desires lead us to the places where we can feel most useful using our gifts and talents.

To use another analogy, you could think of each person as a type of spice in a spice rack. Each has a unique flavor and sense that it brings to whatever it is put into, but any given spice can be used in a wide variety of dishes. And our desire is what guides us toward that type of cuisine that we find the most inviting.

DESIRE QUESTIONS

Networking with many people over the years to figure out their three keys, I have found that a simple set of questions can often clearly bring out the desired component. Read these questions and record your answers:

1. What subject do you never get tired of talking about, even to the point that it annoys your friends?

2. If you had 10 minutes in a bookstore, which you can spend only in one section, which one would it be? Which books would you pick out?

3. If you are up late one night having deep conversations with a couple of friends, what would the topic likely be?

4. But if you are required to take a four-hour class on a topic of your choice, which topic would you choose?

Some people know their interests from the time they are very young. Other people come to be gradually, changing their mind many times along the way. While your design typically stays the same throughout your life, meaning that you always tend to be gifted at certain things, your desire may change significantly over your lifetime. Think about all the things you may have wanted to be when you were younger. Many times they are just phases that you go through. But sometimes something stays with you and becomes a true area of passion. That is what the desire category is all about. If you look at the answers to the questions above, how would you describe what your desire is all about?

Another way to think about it is, where would you like to use your talents? Outside, inside, with lots of people, with just a few people, with children, with older people, with people with certain challenges, with numbers, with ideas? What causes attract and keep your attention, and how would you like to contribute to them?

When you know your design, you know what you are supposed to do; when you learn your desire, you realize where you would like to do it and for whom.

DIAGRAMMING

One of the key elements of an Inspiration is that it has persisted with you over time. Because of that, a great place to start looking for your Inspiration is in your past. What we are searching for is consistent themes — like working with children, animals, books, the sick, those with practical needs; or like a fascination with words or numbers, politics, the environment, making people laugh, foreign cultures, health, etc. Often these passions are sparked by a single event that then becomes a pattern. By looking back, we can see these consistent patterns more clearly. The diagram below is to help you chart out the most important and engaging events and memories from your life.

1. Write in the boxes words or phrases from events that have happened to you that have been the most significant — adventures that captured your imagination, moments you felt like you were at your best and doing what you do well, a favorite class, turning points, favorite skills you used, things you most enjoy doing, etc. They can be in any order and anywhere on the page.

2. Inside or around the boxes, feel free to jot down any of the "why" thoughts about why you picked these moments, what you liked, or disliked about them — what you felt. To what types of careers might they point?

3. When your boxes are filled and you are satisfied you have included everything you want to, look for common themes: teaching people, solving problems, international travel, service, etc. Draw lines between boxes that seem like they go together. Or include them in a list below:

    Theme:

    Theme:

    Theme:

    Theme:

    Theme:

    Theme:

Are there any themes that really surprised you?

Which ones seem the strongest?

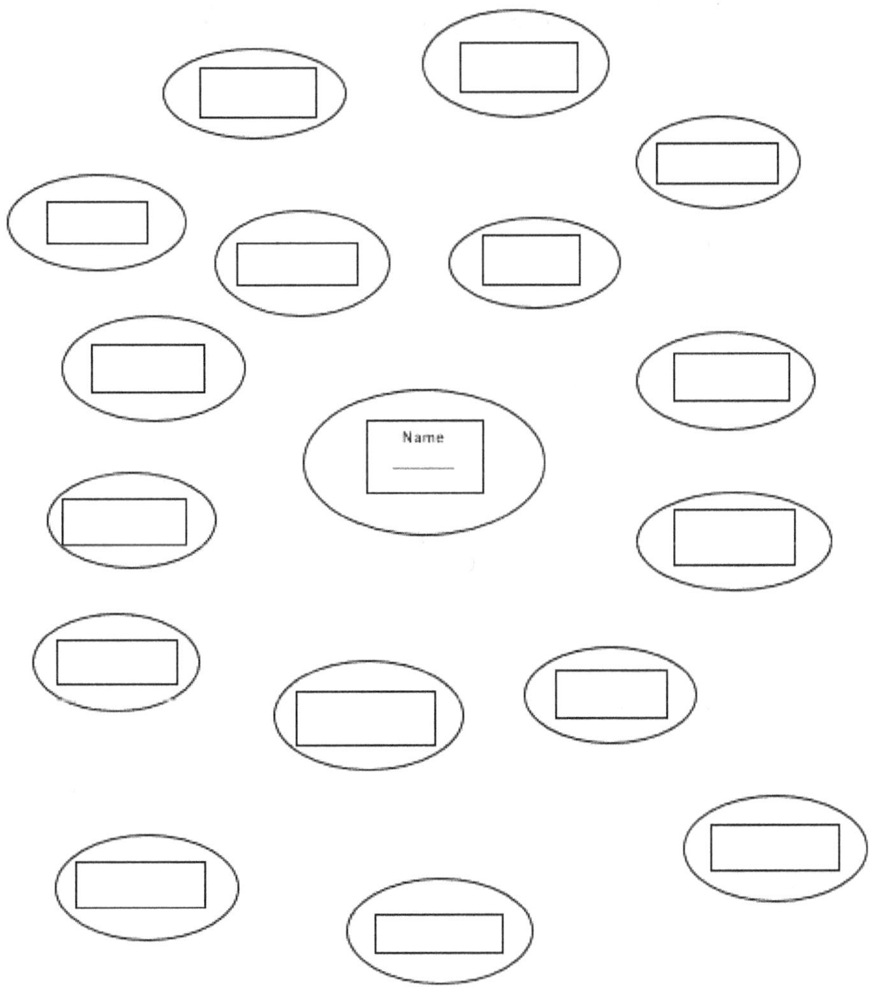

CHAPTER 4:

Discover Your Demand

"Find out what you like doing best, and get someone to pay you for doing it." – Katharine Whitehorn

Okay, so you may have an idea of what you were built to do and some instincts about where to do it. What's next? Well, if you are going to use this combination to make a living, what you are missing is someone who is willing to pay you for it. That is where your demand comes in.

For some careers, the path is obvious. If you have always wanted to be a nurse, or a teacher, or an accountant, or a plumber, there is not a lot of mystery in this part. You need certain training or education and then you apply for clear jobs in the field. In good economies, you may not have to market yourself at all. In weak economies, you just have to show why you are better with the recognized skills than the other people in line.

For many careers, however, it is not this straightforward. That is what makes people nervous. As someone who has worked in colleges for nearly 30 years, I know that so many students choose one of these obvious careers, not because it is either their design or their desire, but simply because they are afraid of the unknown. That is a shame, because it prevents many people from finding something that they could really love.

Despite what people say, the obvious careers are also not foolproof. Although demand tends to be steadier for them, they still see dips. And to me, nothing is sadder, from a career perspective, than to see someone give up their interests for a "safe" career, only to discover that it is not safe.

At the same time, it is important to know that whether you select something with an obvious career path, or a more ambiguous one, you will still have to learn to manage your career. In part, this is because in order to advance in your job, you will have to continue to develop your skills and make yourself stand out. It is also important, though, because people do not stay in the same job for a lifetime much anymore. Even people who go into very traditional positions often find they need a job or career change, even if it is just a change of specialty or focus. This is a lot harder if they have not learned to manage their professional image.

Find Your X

So, what is the key to driving your demand? You have to know your profit per x. What does that mean?

It means that you need to understand what it is that you have to offer that creates value that others want to pay for or support.

For example, if you are a writer, every book or article you publish increases your value, so your equation might be "profit per book." If you are a surgeon, your value might be profit per procedure. If you are an athlete, it might be every championship or medal you earn. This is your value proposition. People do not hire you because you have a degree or because you will show up to work on time. They hire you because you have demonstrated that you can produce something of value for them, so you need to know what that value is.

Think about what you came up with for your design — what were you built to do? And think about your desire — where do you want to do it?

Now ask yourself, who needs this? That is where your demand comes in.

FINDING YOUR DEMAND EXERCISES

One tool to help identify the right career fields for exploration is "Holland Theory." This theory matches up worker characteristics with job category characteristics, demonstrating the areas where people with similar skills tend to find the best job match. Try a simple quiz to figure out your three-letter Holland Code, like the one offered for free at Truity.com.

Don't be thrown off if the jobs it suggests do not match your interests. No test or theory like this can truly tell you what you should be; it serves only to give you ideas of where others who answered similarly found matches. Still, it can be helpful to get you thinking.

The other exploration tool I recommend is the Bureau of Labor Statistics website (www.bls.gov/ooh). This is one of the most comprehensive career information sites available. It provides incredibly in-depth profiles of thousands of jobs and fields. You can look up a specific job and find information on average salary, working conditions, required education and training, projected job outlook, skills needed, and much more. You can search the site many different ways, but one of my favorites is to start with the "Occupational Groups" on the front page. This will help you start narrowing your search to certain fields. If you see jobs you like, select them to see a detailed profile, then click "Similar Occupations" to see related jobs. Using the groups or other search methods (alphabetical, growth rate, education level, etc.), see if you can expand the list of possible careers you may have thought about.

Between possible careers you have already thought about and what you find using these tools, see if you can create a list of six to ten that sound like interesting possibilities.

Write these options down. We will use them as sample careers in an upcoming activity.

CHAPTER 5:

Bringing them All Together

"Your purpose must be particular to you. This is the road less traveled.
Your purpose cannot be someone else's path, not your family's path nor your friends' path." —
Drew Scott Pearlman

Let's think about these three pieces — design, desire and demand — and look at why you need all three together. We will do this by looking at some examples of what happens when you are not working with all three pieces. Admittedly, these will be extreme examples, but I think they will help demonstrate the point.

Case one is "John." John has always been great at math. His parents convinced him he should become an accountant because he is so great with numbers and it is a high-demand field. John makes a great living. He is highly respected in what he does — and he hates it. He is completely bored by looking through people's finances and studying the changes in tax laws. He spends his days waiting for the weekend and dreaming of doing something different.

We see John's design in his excellence with numbers. We see obvious demand for the skills he brings to his work. What we are missing is John's desire. He clearly does not have a passion for what he does, and it is taking a toll on him. Missing just one of the three keys throws the whole system off and keeps him from fulfilling his purpose.

"Ana" loves music. She listens all the time. She can tell you every song on every album of 100 of her favorite musicians. She knows music from lots of categories, attends tons of concerts, and follows the sales figures for all of the chart-toppers. Her dream is to be a musician, preferably in a group, but being a studio singer would also be thrilling. There is only one problem: She's not a very good singer.

Here we have the opposite problem. Ana has a clear desire for what she wants to do. She even knows who pays people to do it. Her challenge is that she does not have the design to support this desire.

"Josh" is an amazing artist. He has always had an artistic flair and a good eye for creating beauty. Over the past few years, he has also developed a strong interest in environmental issues, and especially in supporting recycling efforts. Josh has decided that he will commit himself to creating art out of people's recyclables. He begins to collect items, filling up his garage with trash. He puts together a number of statues, but struggles to make any money because no one seems to want trash sculptures for their parks or buildings.

Silly, I know, but this is clearly a demand problem. Josh has the ability and the interest, but he just has not connected it with anything that people will pay for.

As these rather colorful examples demonstrate, for this to work, we need to get all three keys to work together. When the three are aligned, we begin living from our purpose.

The Three Keys

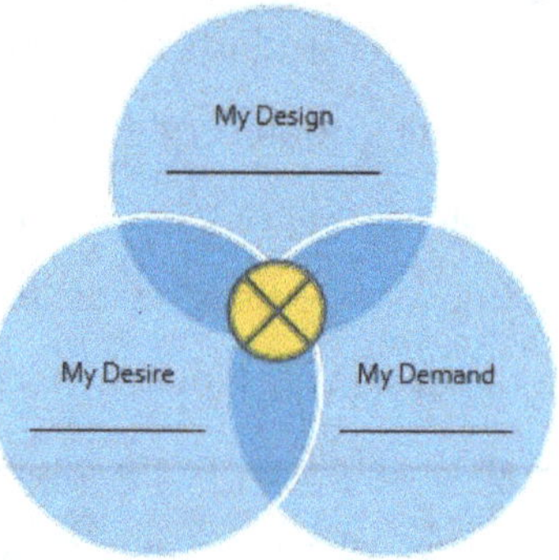

Design tells you who you are and what you should do
Desire tells you where you should do it
Demand tells you how to make a living

CHAPTER 6:

Discover Your Decision-Making Style

"If you have a strong purpose in life, you don't have to be pushed. Your passion will drive you there." — Roy T. Bennett

One of the most helpful tools in your toolbelt when it comes to career planning and job searching is to understand your own decision-making style. This may not seem like a big deal, but not knowing it can make it a lot harder to make good decisions, which can lead you further from your purpose, instead of closer to it.

When you are facing a choice, you need to be confident in the way that you make decisions and not second-guess them. Here is a small quiz to get you started.

0.	I can't always explain why something is the right choice; sometimes I just know.
1.	My decisions make sense and should be clear to anyone.
2.	I sometimes try to convince myself a decision is right, even if it doesn't feel right.
3.	I sometimes wonder why other people have so much trouble making decisions about things that seem obvious.
4.	If I'm struggling to make a decision, I will sometimes ask others their opinion or look for "a sign" about the right choice.
5.	If I'm struggling to make a decision, I will want to do more research because the facts should make the decision clear.
6.	One of the most important considerations is how my decision will affect other people.
7.	What is really important is whether I'm basing my decision on information that is true or false.
8.	The best measure of success for the decisions I have made is that I can look back and feel like I made the right choice.
9.	I can typically measure the success of my decisions in terms of progress toward a goal of mine.

These are all statements that relate to your decision-making style. If you agree with most of the even- numbered statements, you may prefer to make decisions using Feeling (Values). If you relate to the odd-numbered choices, you likely prefer Thinking as a decision-making style.

This difference is important. Thinkers typically have a better career-planning experience if they can objectively weigh the options and have good research to work from. Under stress, they can be tempted to choose rashly, swayed by the emotions of others or uncertain circumstances. Think back to the past: If you have made your best decisions by taking a logical approach, think about how you can apply your logic when making large career decisions.

If you are a Feeling decision-maker, on the other hand, you should not be trying to talk yourself into a decision by building a logical case. Instead, you should examine your deeply held values and then analyze which option most closely aligns to what you truly believe. Feeling people can get themselves into trouble when they receive a lot of advice from well-meaning relatives or co-workers who are Thinkers. They are sometimes convinced by others' logic initially, but once the decision is made they experience regret and frustration because they did not listen to their own inner compass in making the decision. If you are a Feeling person, make sure your gut instinct lines up with "what makes sense" before you choose it.

It can also be helpful to understand your preferred perceiving method. Knowing this will assist you in collecting the right information to make good decisions. Which statements best describe how you collect information about the world?

1.	I notice details and think they are important.
2.	I often miss small details, but I seldom miss the big picture.
3.	Most of my conversations with friends are about things that happen in our daily lives.
4.	Many of my conversations are about ideas I have had or other people have shared with me that I find really compelling. These ideas often stick with me.
5.	Seeing is believing.
6.	Often, what you don't see is more important than what you do.
7.	I prefer the real world to imaginary ones.
8.	Sometimes the real world is not as exciting as the one I envision or read about.

The majority of the population collects information about the world through Sensing. Sensing people are more likely to relate to the odd-numbered statements. Sensors are practical, concrete, and tend to be better with details. If this is you, your career process might benefit from seeing different types of work in action and testing it yourself. Job shadowing and internships could be really helpful. Some Sensing people are more motivated by the working conditions, the benefits, and their daily relationships with their co-workers than they are by the meaning or purpose of the job they are doing. Others want to have a big impact on other people, but typically want to help with their practical needs. Use your senses and try to experience for yourself what jobs will be like.

People who use Intuition to understand the world are less common, but no less important to our complex world. Intuition people see connections in everything. They typically are very motivated by understanding the "why" behind their work. It is essential that they see they are making an impact, even if it may cost them in some of the material benefits of their work. Intuition people use ideas and words to impact the way other people think. Some are very intellectual and driven to change the world of thought. Others are interested in inspiring people and helping them develop their potential. If you are an Intuition person, it is critical that you analyze jobs in terms of what you will be able to change — ideas, people, systems, etc. Will the work capture your thinking, allow you to understand and have influence? Choosing a job that will not feed either your mind or your soul usually results in a bad match.

So, which are you? Thinking or Feeling? Sensing or Intuiting? Use this knowledge to help you in your career decision-making.

CHAPTER 7:

Let's Look at Options

"Figure out what your purpose is in life, what you really and truly want to do with your time and your life, then be willing to sacrifice everything and then some to achieve it. If you are not willing to make the sacrifice, then keep searching." — Quintina Ragnacci

Most people need some time to sit with what they have learned about the three keys. I definitely encourage you to do that. Inspiration does not always come all at once. Sometimes it needs to soak a bit. These are deep themes, and sometimes it will take your brain a bit of time to connect the dots. But usually, with a little time, you will see the picture come together. Incidents from your past will start to fit with your current interests. All those anecdotes your parents love to rehash at Thanksgiving dinner will suddenly make sense.

As you pull the pieces together and begin to evaluate options, it can be helpful to have an organized way to approach the sorting process. I recommend that you try to use a Career Options Matrix to help you rigorously test out your ideas of possible careers.

Here is how it works. Use the format below to list careers you are considering. List these possibilities along the top row. Then, for each possible career, do a quick analysis:

1. How much do I know about this career, on a one-to-ten scale?

   Where are you starting from? How much do you already know about this potential career? Do you know people in this field? Have you read up about it? On the scale of familiarity, where are you starting from?

2. What are the benefits that attract me to this career?

   How does this career fit with your priorities? Does it give you flexibility? Will it support you financially? Does it give you opportunities to travel? What are the positives of this type of position that you already know about?

3. What are the negatives of this field that concern me?

   Have you heard things about jobs in this field that cause you concern? Are there ways that it is in conflict with your priorities? Is it a good match for your design, your desire, and your demand?

4. What would I need to do to start?

   How hard is it to get into this field? Does it require a certain degree, specialized training, or certain types of experiences?

Do you have these qualifications already, or are they something you will need to obtain? Are you willing to put in that work? Can you commit that amount of time and resources?

5. What is my next step for learning more?

    Look at your original knowledge score from question #1. How can you increase that number, especially if it is low? That is to say, if you said that your familiarity with the career is low — say, a 3 — what would it take to get your familiarity to an 8? Can you do some job-shadowing? Can you have a networking conversation with someone in the field? Are there other ways to read, research, or watch videos that will help you increase your knowledge?

6. Now how much interest do I have?

    If you are able to change your level of knowledge and familiarity about the career, what does that do to your interest level? Knowing what you know now, does that make you more or less interested in pursuing this career as an option?

Career Options Matrix

	(Career)	(Career)	(Career)	(Career)	(Career)	(Career)	(Career)
How much do I know about this field? (1-10)							
Benefits of this Field							
Negatives of this Field							
What would I need to do to start?							
Next Step for Learning More							
How much interest do I have? (1-10)							

This is a worksheet you can use throughout your career to make great decisions. If you are considering which field to enter, you can brainstorm a variety of career possibilities to see where to start focusing. When you evaluate the whole list, which options seem more aligned to your goals and your Three Keys?

You can also use this matrix to evaluate a single career choice — for example, by comparing your current situation with the new possibility. You won't always have perfect information, but using this tool can at least help you look carefully at how the two options compare, and it gives you a pathway to make better decisions.

THE PROFESSIONAL DEVELOPMENT TEST

If you've done your homework with the Options Matrix, you should have a short list of career directions you are actively investigating. From your scores, you might even have a favorite that you think is the right fit.

To help you in the narrowing process, or to assist you in confirming you are on the right path, I recommend using a little exercise I call the "Professional Development Test." It is a simple exercise. All that it requires is that you look beyond finding a new career and imagine how you would continue to advance your career five, ten, or fifteen years down the road.

Most jobs require some type of professional development. Some people need to take additional coursework or training, others attend conferences, write articles, serve on committees, take exams, or learn new technologies.

If you want to advance in your field, or even just stay competitive in a changing market, you will need professional development. Knowing this, the key is to ask two questions:

1. What type of professional development is required for the field I am considering?

2. Would I be excited to have this kind of professional development experience on a regular basis?

It is that simple. Professional development is at the heart of growth in each field. It is one of the biggest contributors to your profit equation. If that field is truly a fit for you, you should get excited about at least some of the professional development you have to complete. If you dread the thought of completing it, you are in the wrong field.

If you are thinking about being a scientist, a scholar, or a faculty member, you should enjoy conducting research and writing about it.

If you want to work in the technology industry, you should enjoy learning about and experimenting with new kinds of software.

How would you feel about learning new languages? If you want an international job, that would be a major contributor to your value.

This also works in the negative sense:

- If you don't like giving presentations, don't go into business or public relations.

- If you are not willing to read up on the latest procedures and drugs, medicine is not for you.

- If you will fall asleep listening to new government regulations, skip accounting.

- If you'll go crazy attending training on best policy and procedures, don't aim for social work.

Take the list of jobs from your Options Matrix and test them. Find out what type of professional development is required for advancement in each field by looking at resources like the Occupational Outlook Handbook www.bls.gov/oco. Be honest with yourself. Does the type of training and development necessary sound interesting? Is it something you'd consider learning or doing in your spare time anyway? If you dislike the type of professional development required, you'll seriously limit your success in the field because you won't want to gain new knowledge or network with others who are interested in those subjects.

Use what you learn from this exercise to refine your Options Matrix. If the professional development is a match, consider it a good reason to move that occupation up on your list for research. If not, adjust your interest score accordingly. If you want to love what you do, you need to at least like the tools you need to succeed!

CHAPTER 8:

Managing Your Brand

"If you can tune into your purpose and really align with it, setting goals so that your vision is an expression of that purpose, then life flows much more easily." — Jack Canfield

A brand is a promise that you make to an audience. A personal brand is the promise you make to potential employers — what will you deliver if you are hired?

I am sure you have heard the word "brand" used many times in relation to companies and the way people think about them. The brand is what the company stands for and what it commits to deliver to its customers. What you may not be familiar with is the idea of managing your own personal brand.

What do you stand for? What will you deliver if you are hired for your dream position?

To help communicate this, it is important that you create a professional presence of how you want to be seen. You will want to market yourself as a strong candidate for employers by sending a consistent message of who you are and what you can do.

One of the biggest mistakes that people make in marketing themselves to employers is to focus on features. Features are the things that are observable about you or that you have to offer — like programming capabilities, language skills, strong writing or editing abilities, or years of experience. These are not what sell you to employers.

What really creates value for employers is your benefits.

Benefits are what the employer gets from the features that you offer. For example, your strong writing or editing skills means that the company doesn't need to hire someone else to edit for you, and, in fact, you can help edit others' work to make the organization look good in all of its communication. Your years of experience mean that you will have a shorter learning curve and can become a productive team member much faster than a new person.

See how that works? Here's a visual:

All About Benefits

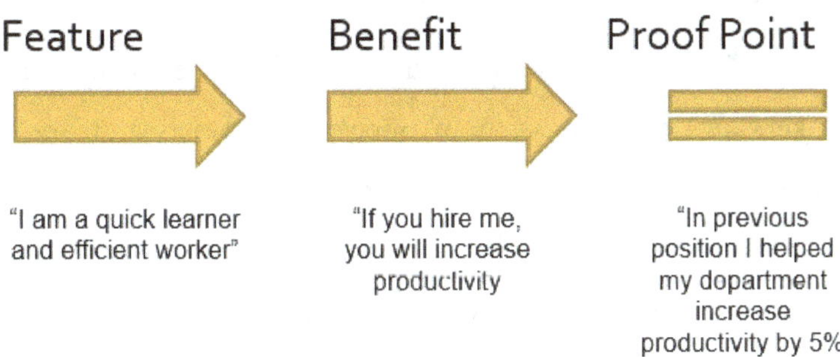

If you want to get good at marketing yourself, make a list of all of the features you think you can offer an employer, and practice turning them around to the employer's point of view. For each feature on your list, come up with the benefit. How does it make the employer's life easier? Does it save them money? Does it save them time? Does it produce happier customers? Reduce complaints? Increase efficiency? Make them look better. Remember, employers make hires to solve a problem. You want to market yourself as the solution to their problem.

What really takes your benefits thinking to the next level is to quantify the benefit. Any time you can use numbers to provide specificity to what you can offer, you immediately strengthen your case. How much have you increased productivity? How much money have you saved? How much revenue have you generated? Quantify what you have done in the past and apply it to possibilities in the feature.

YOUR BRANDING STATEMENT

One of the strongest tools you can have to both get yourself in front of employers and to impress them once you do so is a strong branding statement. A branding statement becomes the centerpiece of all of your marketing tools.

A branding statement will vary in length and content depending on your target audience and the specific circumstances. You might need a short version for introductions, or a classic elevator pitch, but you might want a slightly longer one to use for networking interviews.

In crafting a strong branding statement, consider the following:

- What do you do (job duties)?
- Who do you do it for (stakeholders, customers)?
- Why/how are you good at what you do?
- Why do you like doing it?
- Why are you unique? What's your hook?
- Give proof of how you have done your job well.
- End with a call to action.

You should highlight:
- Your skills
- Your professional attributes
- Your career goals

Your branding statement will likely have multiple uses, including:

- A brand statement (to share verbally)
- Profile statement (to share in writing on your resume)
- Networking statement (to share when asking people to help you network)

Here's an example of a profile statement that I have used on past resumes:

Experienced admissions professional with proven track record of progressive leadership and success in both highly selective and less selective public and private environments. Demonstrated ability to build a successful recruitment team, create a customer service ethos that translates into enrollment success, cultivate strategic relationships, and manage staff and financial resources with integrity and effectiveness. Dedicated to helping institutions achieve long-term enrollment success.

You can think of a branding statement as your "personal commercial" that you can use to effectively advertise yourself to potential employers. To craft a personal commercial:

- Begin with your expertise (not a job title)
- Keep sentences short and simple
- Consider using questions to draw listener in
- Practice it out loud to achieve a relaxed style
- Keep it to 30 seconds, if possible

When you are writing a personal commercial, the goal is to sell. That means being as convincing as possible, using numbers and evidence and creating a sense of energy in the way you present. To give you an idea of what I mean, take a look at these two personal commercials for a professional named Maryanne Jones. The first is the "before" example of how many people write their introductions. The second demonstrates how to add power to your commercial with a few simple adjustments.

***

BEFORE: I'm Maryanne Jones. I am a product/marketing manager with over 17 years of experience in managing products, services, and staff for a corporation. I directed a staff and managed the marketing of all company products.

AFTER: I'm Maryanne Jones. I am a sales-oriented ambassador for companies. For over 17 years, I have created an optimal mix of people, process, and products for company success. I have developed marketing programs for new products, grown the top and bottom line revenue, and increased customer satisfaction.

ACTION ENDING: May I email you a link to my personal website so you can see samples of my work and solutions that I have provided for other companies?

***

Managing your brand involves coordinating the pieces that people see when they look for you. That includes your resume, cover letter, and online presence. It also includes things like how you dress and your phone etiquette. Anything that sends the message that you are an accomplished professional strengthens your brand. You also strengthen it by sharing it with other people — and most importantly, holding up your brand promises.

You can also do damage to your brand by not following through when you say you will or representing yourself in a less-than-professional way. The most common way this happens is through social media posts. People often post things without thinking of the long-term consequences of what they say. In a moment of excitement, it is easy to put something out into the world that will not serve you professionally, so before you fire off that attack email, consider your career.

Need some other ways to promote your brand?

1. Track your accomplishments. I have a sort of "running resume" that I add everything to. I can always go back later and take pieces out that are not relevant, but if you do not record things somewhere, you are likely to forget. All those extras can be helpful. Have you written something, given a presentation, won an award, accomplished a large task, or completed a community service project? Those are all things that can strengthen your brand.

2. Look for training opportunities. Great professionals keep current in their fields. Take advantage of opportunities to add to your knowledge, connect with other professionals, and add to your resume by engaging with training courses, free webinars, and classes that can add to your value. Training that comes with some type of certification is particularly valuable for brand-building.

3. Promote yourself. The career process is one area where you cannot be shy about what you can do. When something good happens, share it with others. Post your accomplishments and comment on others' accomplishments. Create samples of your work to share with people around you. Look for ways to turn lots of eyes in your direction.

4. Become an expert. People pay for expertise. Think of ways

that you can position yourself as an expert in your area. Writing, presenting, being quoted, or recording video are all possible ways to help the world get to know your name.

5. Build relationships. The best way to increase your brand is to keep building good relationships and to grow your network of people who know you, believe in you, and can help you reach your goals.

CHAPTER 9:

Resumes and Cover Letters

"The mystery of human existence lies not in just staying alive, but in finding something to live for." — Fyodor Dostoyevsky

It is easy to find resources that will help you to create a good resume and cover letter. There are many books written on this topic. I will not try to share exhaustively on the topic, but I can give you a few pointers that I have used to help others improve the look and feel of their written materials.

First, I want you to think about resumes and cover letters not as an end in themselves but as a tool to help you get an interview. You don't have to see the product all at once, or share your life's story; you just need to be interesting enough to get the employer to want to know more. This can best be accomplished with a clean, action-oriented presentation that fits your brand and positions you as the answer to the problem the employer is trying to solve.

RESUME TIPS

PROFILE STATEMENT

Some resume coaches and books will suggest that you write an "objective statement" at the top of your resume, especially if you are changing careers or don't have a lot of experience. This would be something like, "To find a marketing position with a company where I can use my social media skills." Honestly, I am not a big fan of these objective statements. Something about them always seems like the candidate is either desperate or lost.

I recommend something instead called a "profile statement." A profile statement is more like a summary of your qualifications that you put into a few sentences.

Here is the one I currently use for my work with colleges:

Experienced enrollment strategist and higher education thought leader with a proven track record of progressive leadership. Enrollment growth and turnaround specialist who has consulted for and advised multiple institutions and higher education companies. Demonstrated ability to lead cross-functional teams across campus to achieve enrollment, retention, career development, and internationalization goals. Fulbright Scholar and international student mobility expert. Quoted four times in Forbes on enrollment topics, published in The Chronicle of Higher Education, University Business, Inside Higher Ed, and the Times Higher Education.

It is a little on the long side, compared to what most people would need, but I have been in the profession for a long time and have a senior position, so for me it makes sense that it is a bit meatier. If you are a young professional, yours might be half that length.

The point is to characterize yourself in the way that you want the employer to think of you. Notice there is no subject of the sentences; they are just descriptive phrases that tell the employer how I see myself and how they should see me. The underlying message is, these are my skills. I have done this for others, and I can do this for you.

Again, you are picking out the highlights of the resume that is to follow, so that if the reviewer doesn't want to read the whole thing, they don't need to. They will know just from your profile who you are and what you have to offer.

This type of profile statement can be really helpful for those individuals who, as we mentioned before, are trying to change fields or just getting started in a field. In a profile statement, you can easily point the reader to the transferable skills you want to highlight. Even if your only work experience is summer jobs or the local coffee shop, you can say something like: "Motivated, responsible team member with a track record of increasing responsibility. Trusted by employers with their fiscal and human resources. Able to multitask in a busy environment and deliver first-class customer service."

PARAGRAPHING

Probably 80 percent of resumes use bullets as their primary tool to convey information. I have to say, I am not a fan. On the one hand, if you have a small number of bullets, say two or three, it does not look that impressive. On the other hand, if your resume is full of long lists of bullets, it uses up a huge amount of your real estate very inefficiently. And, frankly, I think it just looks silly, like you were trying to think of every possible thing you do in your job and adding it to the list.

I much prefer using a paragraphing style. With paragraphing, you use action-oriented phrases, like you did in your profile statement, and you run them together in a block of text. Let me share an example from my resume:

<u>Vice President of Enrollment, Marketing, and Communications</u> 2021-Present

Senior enrollment officer leading a turnaround effort for a comprehensive liberal arts college facing five years of enrollment decline. Manage a staff of 35 in Admissions, Financial Aid, Marketing, Communications, and Graduate Enrollment. Completely overhauled financial aid leveraging and packaging policies. Expanded Early Decision opportunities and more than tripled the number of early decision students in the first year. Launched new international recruitment initiatives that increased international enrollment by 500% in one cycle, and increased international deposits over 700% in the second year. Reinvigorated partnerships across campus to create a multi-division approach to solving enrollment and retention challenges. Strengthened staffing and updated the visit experience. In the first nine months, achieved a 22.3% increase in the freshman class size and a $1.81M increase in overall net revenue.

You'll notice that each phrase starts with a dynamic verb.

Using the paragraphing form gives you more power in less space. Unless you are trying to stretch your resume out because you do not have enough material, I think this is the way to go. It is much more visually pleasing than bullets, and it presents the information in a format that is more familiar to the eye.

NUMBERS

Numbers tell the story more powerfully than words. Often, when you read a resume, it is filled with generalities that can't be measured. They sound good, but they lack specificity or any proof that the person can really deliver.

The way to solve this is to include numbers in your resume. The more you can quantify your results, the more believable they are and the more your reader will attribute them to your actions, instead of thinking you were just in the right place at the right time. When you have your paragraphs written, go back and review them to see if you can quantify something in each assertion you make.

Here is an example:

Director of Admission Services/Senior Associate Dean of Admission
Co-led an enrollment team that transformed a fifteen-year decline into a five-year turn around and unprecedented success for the College. Directed a team that reinvented all aspects of customer service, publications development, programming, outreach, and diversity recruitment. In this five-year period, applications increased by 64% (3425 to 5628), the College's admit rate fell from 62% to 36%, its yield rate increased from 27% to 30%, and the SAT average increased from 1241 to 1300.

In most writing, you would write out the word "percent," but I don't do that with my resumes. The percent sign actually underscores the fact that I'm using numbers and makes them most impactful visually. There are almost always ways you can quantify your assertions more. How many projects do you complete in an average week? How many busy phone lines do you manage? How many calls, on average, do you receive each hour? How many clients do you serve? Adding numbers appeals to the logical part of the reader's brain and recruits it to your side.

HEADINGS AND ORGANIZATION

There are many good ways to format your resume. The important thing is that it is formatted consistently and clearly. It should be easy for the reader to skim down and see what is most important. I like bolded headings that stick out, like "education," "memberships," or "publications." I really like the heading "professional experience," because it allows you to include other relevant items that are not just jobs. You could add training, certifications, volunteer experiences, or other elements that strengthen your expertise in a particular field.

When it comes to employers and job titles, you have two choices.

You can list the employer first and then the title, or you can reverse the order. I typically coach people to lead with whichever is more impressive. If you have good titles from unknown companies, put the title first. If your job titles are forgettable, but you have worked for known companies, consider putting those first.

The important thing is that your resume is easy on the eyes. It should have a few elements that keep it interesting to look at, while still preserving a sense of order and consistency.

Educational Credentials
- U.S. Fulbright International Education Administrator Award – Japan   2015
- *Master of Arts in History* (Latin America), University of Illinois at Urbana-Champaign   1997
  Foreign Language and Area Studies Fellow (FLAS)
- *Bachelor of Arts International Studies*, Summa Cum Laude, West Virginia Wesleyan   1996
  Wesleyan Scholar, Truman Scholar Finalist
- Rotary Exchange Scholar, Instituto Dr. Alexis Carrel, Rio Tercero, Argentina   1993
- MBTI and Enneagram Certified

PROOF IT

It is critically important to have your resume proofread. Resumes are not the form of reading we are most used to, so mistakes tend to stand out more easily. Employers can easily infer from errors on a resume that you are sloppy with your work, which is definitely not a conclusion we want them to draw!

One of my favorite "extras" for your writing is to eliminate the fluff. It is amazing how many additional words we add into our writing to soften or qualify it. Not all of these words are necessary for the meaning, and in many cases, they actually detract from the clarity of communication. When you have your resume written, go back and eliminate any word that does not add value to the sentence. You will be impressed by how much better this makes your writing. Less is more in this case.

COVER LETTER TIPS

While your resume sells your skills and capabilities, your cover letter provides the personality to your application. A good cover letter is made up of three parts — an introduction, two highlights and a closing. Some people write very long cover letters. I don't think that is necessary, unless you are asked to share specific items. My philosophy is to write what you need to get the job done, but don't look like you are trying too hard.

Your first paragraph is an introduction. Here you often state why you are interested in the position, where you heard about it, and a request for consideration.

"Please accept this letter of application for the position of Assistant Vice President of Enrollment Management, posted on September 14th. I believe that my experience and demonstrated commitment to seeing (University) achieve healthy, competitive enrollment make me an excellent fit for this opportunity."

The second paragraph should typically highlight the strongest reason that you would be a good fit for the position. I typically focus on the tangibles of the match between the position and my skills. I talk about my years of experience, my most outstanding results, and any recognition I have received from it.

"I can offer the University fourteen years of progressive leadership in the admissions field at three different institutions. At each, I have helped the organization achieve the highest levels of enrollment success in its history. During the last six years, I have actively participated in the design and implementation of financial aid models that have leveraged scarce institutional dollars to maximize both student profile and net

tuition revenue. I have paired this experience with an interest in seeing students develop professionally by teaching the Personal Career Management course for the past two years.

During that time, I have assisted Career Services with student advising, workshop presentations, and the launch of several new technology initiatives."

Paragraph three is similar to paragraph two, but highlights another aspect you would bring to the position. This can be a second skill that would add value or another aspect of your experience. I like to use this as my "passion paragraph." Here, I balance out the logic in paragraph two with my motivation for working in the field, or what attracts me about this position specifically. I think it is a nice contrast.

"I have long contended that true enrollment management is not limited to the years that a student takes classes, but extends from the first contact the prospective student has with a university to the student's successful transition to the world of work. Part of what makes this position such an attractive opportunity for me is the combination of departments that it represents, and the chance to build a comprehensive enrollment vision from the collaboration of Admissions, Financial Aid, and Career Services. (University) has achieved great success in its traditional undergraduate enrollment in the last few years and now has the opportunity to integrate areas like graduate enrollment, international enrollment, student outcomes, and sustainable financial aid planning into a more unified enrollment model. I would be honored to help the University achieve this goal."

In paragraph four, you are just going for a graceful closing. For some reason, this is often the hardest part to write. Everyone knows you are just trying to close. Some people indicate their interest in next steps or provide contact information. Those are all fine. The goal of this paragraph is just to close out the letter without saying anything awkward.

> *"I look forward to the opportunity to further discuss the Assistant Vice President position. Please contact me at (phone) or (email) if I can provide more information about the experience, energy, and leadership I would bring to this pivotal role."*

Stick to this format and keep it simple.

With these two documents, you are ready to whet the appetite of any hiring manager and make them want to learn more!

CHAPTER 10:

Networking

"If you can tune into your purpose and really align with it, setting goals so that your vision is an expression of that purpose, then life flows much more easily." — Jack Canfield

Some people get very nervous about the idea of networking. They imagine a crowded room in which they have to glad hand and be the life of the party. This is not the case. You do not have to be an extroverted person to be great at networking, nor do you have to be pushy.

Networking is nothing more than building relationships with people who would be inclined to help you in your career management. It is often done one-on-one in a very relaxed way. In fact, that is the way it usually works best. The basic concept of networking is that the more people who know about what you are looking for, the more likely you are to uncover new opportunities.

One of the very best ways to network is to ask people about the work that they do. This is often referred to as informational interviewing. Informational interviewing is one of the most powerful tools that you have to find job opportunities and recruit people to help you succeed. Luckily, it is also usually a pretty pleasant experience.

It works like this. Identify individuals you know, or that your friends or relatives know, who work in or close to the field that you are pursuing. Let them know that you are researching careers in their area and wonder if they would be willing to share their experience and help you gain insight about what the work entails and how to best prepare for jobs in that area. If they say yes, meet with them or set up a conversation — maybe over coffee or lunch (everyone has to eat).

Do not pressure them about anything; simply ask them to share their experience. What do they like about the work they do? What do they not like? How did they get into the field? What advice would they have for someone trying to start in that area? You should bring a copy of your resume in case they ask to see it. If they do not, you can always ask if they would be willing to take a look, or if you could send it to them later. Toward the close of the conversation, ask them if they know other people they think you should talk with to gather more information.

That's it (although I suggest you follow up with a thank-you note).

Usually, one of two things will happen. Either the person will be happy to fill you in about their experience and give you a few suggestions and wish you good luck. In this case, you may not have discovered any new leads, but you have recruited another person to be on the lookout for good opportunities for you. On the other hand, the person may really warm up to your cause. They may begin networking for you, thinking about people who might have openings, sharing their contacts, or offering to reach out and make introductions for you.

Either of these outcomes is a win, so no need to push. Enjoy the conversation, take good notes, and thank the person sincerely for thinking through things with you.

You can see how this tool is powerful. It allows you, in a relaxed setting, to build a relationship that spreads your network at the same time that it increases your understanding of the job field. You pick up new jargon from the profession, add to your contacts, and learn what kinds of people can open doors for you.

NETWORKING PRESENTATION

Just as you have a branding presentation that you can use to introduce yourself to employers, it can be helpful to have a networking presentation that you use when approaching people related to the industry, but who may be in a more information-giving role. Look at this example template that you can adjust to fit you:

My name is J(name). I currently work as a (function) <u>professional</u> in the (industry). Most recently, I have served as (level, functional title) at <u>Company Name,</u> a (description of organization if helpful).

During my career I have developed skills and strengths in (skill #1), (skill #2), and (skill #3). I'm currently exploring new career opportunities because (reason). I am looking for an opportunity to use my (skill), (skill), (skill) skills in an area such as (example).

I am interested in talking to people in (X industry) to learn as much as I can about what companies in this field need. With your expertise, can you provide me with some insight into the industry? Are there people you think I should talk with to increase my industry knowledge and help me to be the strongest candidate possible?

LINKEDIN, THE NEW NETWORK

If you are not actively using LinkedIn to help manage your career, you are really missing out! It is so powerful. LinkedIn serves many functions for professionals. First, it is a way to store your contacts, but it is also a way to keep up with them and nurture them in ways that were so much harder before it was created.

In the "old days," people used a Rolodex, a business card holder that you could flip quickly to the phone number you needed. To maintain relationships, you would need to call your contacts on a rotating schedule. Now you can easily follow along with the updates of everyone in your LinkedIn contacts.

LinkedIn also allows you the ability to always be in the job market. On your profile, you can highlight your skills, share your work philosophy, and show samples of your work, awards, and accomplishments. And no one thinks it is strange that you are constantly marketing yourself to employers and colleagues.

LinkedIn also offers amazing ways to build your network. Not only does it suggest new contacts to you, but you can research the contacts of people you are connected to, and either contact them or ask the person you know to give you an introduction. You can also use some of its more advanced search features to help you identify people with whom you have things in common. For example, you can find other graduates of your college or university, or look for people who also worked at companies where you have worked.

LinkedIn will also bring information to you. If you follow companies, you will receive job postings and updates of events and new initiatives. If you join groups, you can get tips and meet people who can help you. LinkedIn will even pitch you postings of jobs it thinks match your profile.

Linkedin is a recruiter's dream, so make sure you are taking full advantage of this amazing machine.

There are entire books written about how to maximize your effectiveness on LinkedIn. I will not duplicate that work here, but I will make a few quick suggestions:

1. Complete your profile: A robust and well-thought-out profile shows that you take your professional development and career seriously.

2. Ask people in your network for recommendations: Anytime people are making a purchase, peer reviews matter. Having a few well-written recommendations on your profile inspires confidence.

3. Add samples: If you have examples of your work that you feel are particularly strong, share them. Consider them an electronic business card.

4. Post occasionally: You do not need to be constantly adding content to your feed, but do share accomplishments, articles, and updates so that people know you are alive and active on LinkedIn. Keep your posts upbeat but professional.

CHAPTER 11:

Interviews

"Perhaps the single most important ingredient in all of life for achieving happiness and fulfillment — purpose." — Harvey Volson

I am one of those weird people who actually really likes to do job interviews. I find them exciting. You meet new people, learn new things — and people say a lot of nice things about you!

Interviewing is about reading people and situations. It is knowing how much to share and what not to share. Some people interview naturally, but whether you do or not, you can learn techniques and approaches that will help you improve both your success and your comfort in interview situations.

KNOWING WHO YOU ARE

Employers appreciate candidates who have done some self-analysis and self-reflection. This is another way that using the Three Keys method can help you. The work you have done to discover your design, your desire, and your demand also serve you to more confidently talk about yourself in your cover letter or interview. You know where your gifts lie, you know what motivates you, and you know the difference you can make in the world. You also know your value, which will help you more easily answer questions and adjust, no matter where the conversation goes. Take what you have learned about yourself and make them part of your brand and the way you present yourself.

KNOW WHAT YOU WANT

Your self-analysis will also help you to know what you want and to be able to talk about it with confidence. You will know you do not have to take any job that comes your way. Instead, you can set some guidelines that will help you find something that fits your desire and the vision you have.

Think about past work you may have done and note the specific aspects of it that you found satisfying. What parts did you most enjoy and why? What projects gave you the biggest sense of accomplishment? What was it about the position that made it most enjoyable? Can you look for those elements in your next position?

Use what you learn from this analysis to prepare interview questions that will help you determine if the next job opportunity is a good fit for you. Go beyond the job title to probe into what the true duties look like. What does an average day entail? What energizes people about this position? What drains them?

Being open about what you are looking for (without sounding like you think you are entitled to it) can be a great way to avoid "dating syndrome." This is when candidates interview for positions and both the candidate and the employer oversell themselves as perfect. Candidates try to mold themselves to what they think the employer wants and employers paint an overly rosy picture of what they are offering.

What usually happens is that both are disappointed and the match does not last long.

USING THE SAR METHOD

One way to tackle both your cover letter and interviews is to utilize what is called the "SAR Method" (Situation Action Result). This approach utilizes examples of situations to demonstrate the proof of what you are able to do.

- What was the problem (problem, situation, project) at the time?
- What <u>specific</u> actions did you take to solve the problem, overcome the challenge?
- What were the results? (for you, the company, the team)

- Provides easy method of remembering <u>how</u> to tell your story.
- Gives evidence of your strengths and skills.
- Builds your sense of self worth.
- Helps others remember you.
- Provides a direct link to your marketing campaign.

- Write a brief SAR story that you can present in one or two minutes.
- <u>Position</u> your SAR statement with an introductory line, such as:
"One of my strengths is the ability to _______________." *Or*
"My strength in cost containment is best illustrated by an example."

My success rate at interviews is pretty high, but it is because I have discovered some practices that really work for me. You can develop a system that works for you based on your strengths as well, but here are some tips that I think anyone can employ (pun intended).

Arrive Early

Whenever I am going to an interview, I arrive close to the location early. To me, the worst feeling is to arrive late to something like an interview because I have gotten lost. I often go early, make sure I lay eyes on the location, and then go get coffee or breakfast somewhere nearby. Worst-case scenario, I can walk to the interview spot. I try to arrive 5-10 minutes early for the interview. I don't want to be there before that, especially if it starts at the beginning of the day. I want to make sure people are ready for me, but that they are not waiting for me.

Come Prepared

Preparation is your best friend in interview situations. This is an area that many people struggle with. I think they are unsure how to prepare.

I would first check the employer's website to see if they share much information about their corporate values, their structure, or their current important projects. If you can find an organizational chart, I would print it out and bring it with you. Note what language is used as part of the corporate culture. If there are bios for important leaders at the company, read them over. If you can find any kind of strategic plan, take the time to at least skim it to get an idea of what the company is officially committed to doing.

Most of the questions, however, probably will be about you, so it is more important that you know how to speak about yourself and to be able to talk about how you have handled situations in the past. My secret weapon has always been to create a list of the questions that I think I am likely to be asked and actually write out my answers to those questions.

This isn't difficult to do. Google can easily provide you with the most common interview questions. Pick 15-20 and write out responses. For example, it is highly likely that you will be asked:

1. Why are you interested in this position?

2. What are your strengths and weaknesses?

3. Tell us about a time when you had to demonstrate (leadership, resilience, creativity, resourcefulness, etc.)?

4. How do you handle stress/pressure?

5. Where do you hope to be five years from now?

6. Tell us about a time that you made a mistake and what you did about it?

These are all standard questions, and there are a few more that almost always appear in one form or another during an interview. Why would you go into an interview cold when you can predict much of what you will be asked?

If you take the time to write out the answers to these questions, you will not be scrambling on the spot to think of good examples. The bonus is that preparing ahead of time not only allows you to answer these exact questions, but it allows you to extrapolate to other similar questions. For example, let's say you prepare for the strengths and weaknesses question. Maybe your interviewer will not ask that, but instead something like, "Tell us one area you would like to grow," or "What are the primary skills you can bring to our team?" Can you see how these are just other forms of the same question? If you already have an answer mapped out about your strengths and weaknesses, your brain will automatically tap into it to answer these related questions. There really are only a small number of actual topics you are likely to get questions about, even though the questions may be formulated differently.

I like to write out my list of questions as early as possible. Then I spend much of my prep time reviewing them. I don't fully commit them to memory, so that they don't sound rehearsed (I don't think I could anyway), but I familiarize myself with them enough that they come to mind easily when I'm asked that kind of question. This technique probably has been my number one confidence-builder in interview situations.

PREP QUESTIONS

You need a list of questions that you want to ask going into an interview. Sometime in the last portion of the interview you will almost always be asked, "What questions do you have for us?" It is always an awkward moment when a candidate says, "None."

Many people make the mistake of preparing only two or three questions. This might be okay if you are only going to meet with one person or group, but often you will be introduced to an interview by multiple people at multiple levels. Sometimes one person will accompany you to all of these meetings. You need to have enough relevant questions to get you through the day.

The safest question to start with is something that reinforces that if you are selected, you will excel. Ask what true success will look like for this position in the first sixty to ninety days. Ask what are the most important characteristics the successful candidate will need to be a home run-hitter for the organization. You want to signal that you intend to not just show up, but to contribute and make the institution look good.

If you need a safe question to fill some time, ask if anyone can share their favorite thing about working there, or their biggest challenge. This invites participation from the group and shows that you care what other people think.

As with common interview questions, you can easily ask Google to help you with a list of good questions to ask. One that not many people think of, but I have always been impressed by, is to ask near the end, "What haven't you asked me that you would really like to ask?" This is a great way to tease out any underlying doubts that people might be hesitant to vocalize. If you can bring them to the surface, you have a chance to address concerns that could negatively impact you in the process.

TAKE NOTES

This might sound like a small thing, but bring a padfolio with you. This can help you in all kinds of ways. If I know ahead of time who I will be meeting with, I make a page for each meeting. I write relevant bullet points from my pre-prepared questions and the questions for me to ask that I think might be most relevant. I also typically tuck my pre-prepped question sheet into the portfolio side.

I will often ask, "Is it okay if I take a few notes?" That gives me an excuse to consult my sheets or refer to my list, should I need to. When I am asked if I have any questions, I answer "yes" and consult my list, which helps me look prepared.

Having this kind of padfolio also allows you to jot down the names of the people in the room you are meeting with. I often find this the hardest part. When you are nervous, names easily get away from you, so I try to put them in the order of the people at the table in case I forget. Taking notes is also a good way to take a breather to collect your thoughts.

TAKE A PAUSE

At some point during the interview, you will likely be asked something you don't expect. Don't panic. You should not have stock answers for everything. In fact, interviewers will sometimes get a little worried if candidates answer too glibly, or charge blindly ahead with answering before they think. When you are asked something that you are not ready for, try saying something like, "Wow, that's a great question." You can even follow it up with, "Let me think about that for a moment." That gives your brain a moment to process and access better examples. Interviewers will not take this badly. In fact, it shows that you are thoughtful about your answers, which is generally what they would like from their employees. Think about how much damage could be avoided if employees were more thoughtful before pushing the "send" button on some of their emails!

SEND A THANK YOU

It might sound old-fashioned, but people do appreciate "thank-you" notes, and they do pay attention to them. Today it is more common to send a thank-you email than a handwritten note, but whatever form it takes, a follow-up thank you does make a difference. Besides, following through is part of your brand, right? This is why you'll be happy you took notes on people's names. It does make a difference. So, make your mom happy and send a thank you.

CHAPTER 12:

After the Interview

"It is not enough to have lived. We should be determined to live for something."
- Winston Churchill

It is not uncommon to have multiple interview rounds, depending on the level of the position. Especially with the common use of virtual meetings, companies often use an initial screening interview before an on-site visit. Sometimes it is all virtual.

Usually, companies will check your references before making an offer, but it has become more and more common for them to reach out to your reference list earlier in the process. Sometimes this happens before an in-person visit. Usually, the company will let you know if they plan to do reference checks early in the process, but every employer is different.

In assembling a reference list, you obviously want to choose people who know you well and can speak to your strengths. Employers will put more emphasis on people who have worked directly with you. In most cases, they will be interested in your direct supervisors. This can be tricky if you are currently in a job and do not have a great relationship with your supervisor, or if you don't want your company to know you are looking.

I have been in this situation before. What I typically do is list people who I know will give me strong references and who have gone on to higher titles. If possible, I also list previous supervisors so that employers can say they have spoken with my boss, even if it is not my current boss. If the employer wants to speak to my current boss, I ask them to wait until I am a finalist or their final candidate and then say that I would like a chance to speak with my boss first. Generally, there is some understanding of the awkwardness of this position. Many people have been in this exact situation, and everyone else can imagine how it would be if they were in your place.

Your reference list can be a short document — just one page. I typically list four references, in case the employer cannot reach one right away. I always reach out to my references before I start a new search to make sure they are still willing and that I still have their correct contact information. I also keep them updated when I have a position I will be interviewing for; that way, if they get a request, they have a better idea of what the position is about. References are almost always asked the same kinds of questions as well, so it can be worthwhile to make sure they are comfortable talking about your strengths and weaknesses.

RECEIVING AN OFFER

Hopefully, all of this hard work has paid off and you receive an offer for the position. Obviously, a salary offer will be part of the conversation. There is a lot of good information available on how to negotiate salaries. Some people love to negotiate; other people hate it. You need to do what feels right to you.

If you decide to negotiate, remember to do so with class. This is probably someone you will need to work with in the future, so you don't want the first impression to be one that makes them think they have made a mistake. Here are some possible types of responses:

- First, always thank them for the offer and reiterate that you are excited about the opportunity.

- You can pause for a few seconds to indicate you are surprised or considering, and see if they offer something different.

- You can ask if they have any flexibility.

- You can indicate you were hoping "for something more like... ."

- You can offer something that does not hurt you, like starting early or working some extra hours when you start.

- If you sense they can't move on salary, you can ask for other benefits that are easier for them to give.

- You can reflect back what they have told you about the importance of the position and encourage them that you will be worth the extra investment.

If you would like strategies on how to better negotiate, I highly recommend the book, *Never Split the Difference*, by former FBI negotiator Chris Voss.

When you have clarified the salary and details, you can accept on the spot or ask for an overnight to think about it, depending on how big a move you are making.

I always encourage candidates to be careful to maintain their brand during the period between the offer and when they start the new position. Hopefully, the company will be excited about your start and accommodating as you make the change, but don't assume that. Make sure that you communicate well, but drag the hiring manager into your personal dynamics. Accept help if it is offered, but don't expect special treatment. You want to arrive on day one with everyone just as excited as they were on the day you were hired, so keep things professional and positive.

CHAPTER 13:

Assessments

"The meaning of life is to find your gift. The
purpose of life is to give it away."
— Pablo Picasso

Assessments can be a great tool to help you make sure that you are on the right path with your career exploration. I have used many assessments in the past and figured out which ones work for me. When I do career advising, I almost always recommend that people take some time and use certain assessments to get to know themselves better. Here are a few assessments that I would recommend:

THE KEIRSEY TEMPERAMENT SORTER: (WWW.KIERSEY.COM)

One of the easiest to use, and yet most effective, personality approaches is "Temperament Theory." Temperament Theory was first proposed by David Keirsey, but he points to a long historical tradition of dividing people into four categories by their personality styles. These four patterns dictate how individuals typically interact with the world.

Keirsey points to two main questions that determine one's

temperament: 1) Does the person use concrete language or abstract language? and 2) When the person tries to get a job done, does he or she use only approved tools and only in a cooperative way, or any tools necessary to get the job done?

That's it. No complex testing necessary. No ink blots or couch sessions. Just two questions. That is what makes this theory so portable and accessible.

So, what do these questions mean? First, listen to the people around you talk. What do they talk about and how do they say it? Some people focus on the here-and-now. They talk about visible, practical things that you can see, hear, or touch. In a 20-minute conversation with them, you will hear about the new pair of jeans they bought, what they ate for lunch, what they will be doing that afternoon, and what someone said to so-and-so about such-and-such. These are the concrete things they care about.

With others, in a 20-minute conversation you will hear about the latest movie they saw and how it really makes them wonder about the future of technology. You might discuss a theory they have about how some major issue could be resolved, or ponder what an event means. They easily see comparisons between ideas or events and they often try to figure out where an event "fits into" the bigger picture.

The first group contains concrete language users. The people in the second group are abstract language users.

For question two, you have to understand how Keirsey uses the word "tool." In Temperament Theory, a tool is anything that can be manipulated to accomplish something. Construction workers may use hammers or saws, athletes may use their bodies, musicians use instruments or voices, marketers use slogans, diplomats use foreign languages — all these are things I can learn to use to bring about a desired outcome.

But how do I choose to use them? Cooperatives play by the rules when they use tools. They are careful to do things in a way that is socially acceptable. They care about how their actions are perceived. They want to be seen as fair and kind. They generally value harmony in interactions, but more important than harmony, they think everybody should be using the same playbook.

Their opposites (Keirsey calls them the Utilitarians) think this is dumb. Why would you observe arbitrary rules if something else would be more effective? Why should people's feelings be more important than what works? You can easily see this dynamic at work. Get a group of people working on a task and see who wants to cooperate and who wants results first.

Combine these two questions and you get four unique quadrants that provide a powerful tool for understanding motivation.

Here's an example. The time is 6:37 PM. I'm in a group of people and one of them asks me, "What time is it?" I say, "6:30." Someone else corrects me and says, "No, it is 6:37." The cooperatives in the group might become indignant. Half of them (abstract cooperatives) are concerned that I am messing with the harmony of the group environment, and the other half (concrete cooperatives) see it as "something you just don't do" for good social etiquette. The Utilitarians, on the other hand, would wonder why I had rounded off, and back the person who corrected me. Half of them (abstract utilitarians) would be concerned "for the sake of accuracy" and the other half (concrete utilitarians) would think I was being wishy-washy by giving a vague number.

Want to test this out? Ask a group of friends to play a game with you and let tempers flare a little. Who wants to quit when the rules aren't followed, and lets others win if they keep playing? (concrete

cooperatives) Who is willing to change the rules if everyone agrees to it and we're all learning together? (abstract cooperatives) Who is happy for a change in the rules, or to exploit a loophole if it is to their advantage, or just generally seems more effective? (concrete utilitarian). Who wants to play using the more advanced set of rules no one else is familiar with, and is secretly masterminding a takeover of the game? (abstract utilitarian).

MYERS-BRIGGS TYPE INDICATOR

The "Myers-Briggs" system may be the most famous personality inventories. This system breaks people into 16 personality types based on opposite pairs of characteristics. You've certainly heard of people referred to as extroverts or introverts. This is the first pair of features used by Myers-Briggs. People who are introverts create their own internal energy, usually by spending time by themselves, or perhaps with just one or two other people. People who are extroverts draw their energy from other people, and often enjoy being surrounded by others.

The second pair of features asks whether a person prefers to use their senses or their intuition. Sensory people observe the world around them and come to conclusions based on what they can see, feel, smell, taste, etc. Intuitive people look at the world around them to find meaning using their intuition.

They look for connections between things, relationships, and things that may be unspoken and are not as obvious. These are the two ways that people collect information about their world.

The third set of characteristics has to do with the way that people make decisions. Thinking people tend to use logic to decide the best course of action. They look at the facts and do not consider much how those facts might influence or impact other people. Feeling decision-makers, on the other hand, focus on the outcome of a certain decision on themselves and the people around them. They tend to base their decisions on values, rather than using logic.

Finally, some people have a strong desire to see things resolved and make their decisions quickly, while other people prefer to keep their options open and allow things to develop before making a firm decision. The first category of people are Judgers They are more comfortable when a decision is made and they are able to move forward on it. The second group are called Perceivers This group wants to know their options before committing themselves.

These four sets of characteristics combine in different ways to produce the 16 personality types. If you know your type, you can gain a lot of insight into the way you interact with other people and the way that you perceive and act in your world.

Here is the set of four preference pairs from myersbriggs.com:

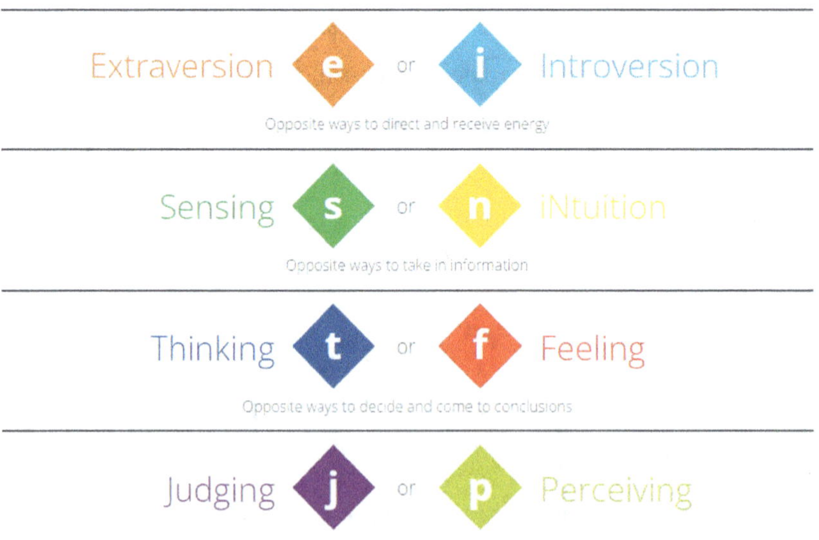

The Myers-Briggs system is well developed and gives a lot of insight.

For me, it is not as helpful in career- specific decisions as it is in understanding your personality in the way that you interact with other people.

THE ENNEAGRAM

The "Enneagram Assessment" has been one of my favorites the past couple of years. It has its champions and its detractors, but for me it has been a useful concept. The Enneagram shows us what is out of balance in a person's life. It indicates our motives — the *why* behind the personality we display. "Enneagram" comes from the word for "nine" and "figure," and indeed, the Enneagram concept is displayed as a set of interrelated personality types around a nine-sided diagram. These personalities represent nine ways that we learn to confront the world, as well as our primary strategy for trying to meet our own needs for acceptance and security.

The Enneagram usually shows you what you don't want to see about yourself — the mask you most frequently hide behind. As author Ian Morgan Cron suggests, however, this is not a negative: "The Enneagram doesn't put you in a box. It shows you the box you're already in and how to get out of it." (Cron, *The Road Back to You: An Enneagram Journey to Self-Discovery)*

The way I like to think about it is that when we are very young, we experience stressful situations and we find a strategy that seems to work to handle those situations. When the world doesn't make sense, we use that strategy to understand it. Unlike most systems, the Enneagram tends to look at what our weaknesses are and the ways that we would default to certain behaviors. Some people see that as negative, but I find it extremely insightful.

The concepts behind the Enneagram go back several thousand years, at least to the geometry of Pythagoras, and likely through Sufi and Judaic mystic traditions. It was introduced as a human development system to the West by George Gurdjieff in 1915, and was picked up by priests in the Catholic Church, who used it as a tool for individual counseling and self-awareness. It has since spilled over to other faith-based organizations, including a number of colleges and universities, who offer it to their students. It also has found its way into industry. According to a research team from Cal State, Stanislauss, ((PDF) The Enneagram and Its Possibilities for Student Learning (researchgate.net)) the Enneagram has been used by executives at Motorola, Boeing, Toyota, AT&T, Adobe, and Marriott. Even the CIA has used it to profile international leaders.

There are nine types of personalities represented by the Enneagram. Each personality speaks to a particular need that type of person has. Type one is the need for perfection, type two is the need to be needed, the type three has the need to succeed, type four the need to be different, type five has the need to guard one's own energy, type six the need for security, type seven the need for distraction and to avoid pain, type eight the need to fight against something, and type nine the need to avoid or to find peace. If you understand each of these needs, you can see how people are motivated to act in the ways that they do, and you can see why certain people's needs are in conflict with each other.

With even a basic understanding, it won't take long to look around a workplace and see these needs everywhere. The administrative assistant who helps people look like they have their act together, never forgets anyone's birthday, and knows how to get things done behind the scenes is probably a number two "Helper." The faculty member who is so good at finding the flaw in every idea and observing in a detached way, but resists committing his own time, energy, and ideas, may be a number five

"Investigator." The person who seems to steamroll everyone and argues with you even when you are trying to agree with her might be an eight "Challenger." And there is a reasonable chance that the new employee who dyes her hair a different color each week and seems to just invite others to pick on her is a four "Individualist."

Each type also has what is called a "type dynamic." For example, a three (the need to achieve) under a lot of stress will act more like a nine (the need to avoid), letting important things go without a fight, or becoming lethargic and falling asleep to life. A three who feels confident and secure will start to act like a well-adjusted six, enjoying loyal friendships and making time for the simple pleasures of life.

Understanding these dynamics can be just as valuable to your team members as knowing their type, especially during stressful times. People can learn to recognize the signs of stress and burnout in themselves before they take them out on others, or before they give up on the environment and leave.

I have used the Enneagram successfully in group and team dynamics. But it also has been the system that probably has helped me the most to understand my own motivations, so it is worth a look.

OTHERS

There are many other systems that can be useful. Earlier I mentioned the Holland codes — three letter codes that described the types of skills and interests that people most enjoy using. This can be a very simple, concrete way to think about job categories and job types. You can easily find Holland assessment by using a search engine.

I've also recently been impressed by the "Working Genius" system for understanding team dynamics. It looks at the project delivery process as a set of steps that requires people with different skills to be able to perform and bring things to completion. I recently took this assessment and saw some of my own team dynamics and team contributions in a new light, so I would recommend it as well.

But one of the most popular assessments at the moment is the "Clifton Strengths Test." I've seen this used successfully by individuals and organizations. This assessment helps you to find your five top strengths out of a list of 34. It encourages you not to try to fix your deficiencies, but to focus on maximizing your strengths. This can be an excellent tool to help you in the workplace to figure out where you can make the best contribution, and how you can utilize your strengths to propel your career forward.

The 34 Clifton Strengths are divided into four domains, which are listed below from the Gallup website.

STRATEGIC THINKING

- Analytical
- Context
- Futuristic
- Ideation
- Input
- Intellection
- Learner
- Strategic

RELATIONSHIP BUILDING

- Adaptability
- Connectedness
- Developer
- Empathy
- Harmony
- Includer
- Individualization
- Positivity
- Relator

INFLUENCING

- Activator
- Command
- Communication
- Competition
- Maximizer
- Self-Assurance
- Significance
- Woo

EXECUTING

- Achiever
- Arranger
- Belief

- Consistency
- Deliberative
- Discipline
- Focus
- Responsibility
- Restorative

Test these assessments to see which ones work best for you. They all have value, but some people relate better to some than others. Having a framework that speaks to you can go a long way in helping you make great career choices.

CHAPTER 14:

Managing Your Career for Life

"Knowing your purpose gives your life meaning, simplicity, focus, and motivation. It also prepares you for eternity." — Rick Warren

You now have the tools you need, not just to find your next job, but the one after that, and the one after that. You now have what you need to manage your career for life.

Start by confirming your design. Spend the time to look into your past and understand who you are and what you are meant to do. Make sure, at each fork in the road of your career, you are testing the options to see if they are a better or worse fit for your design. This should be your North Star.

Continue to monitor your desire. Unlike your design, this is likely to change significantly over time. You will develop new passions that will call to you. This is good. Just make sure that when you find an area of desire, you plug into it in a way that leverages your design. Desire will not be enough to carry you and make you successful; you need to be a match as well.

Keep your eyes on the market to make sure you always stay in demand. Invest in your professional development. Learn new skills, get additional credentials, and stay current in your field. If you are in the right place, this kind of professional development will not be a heavy burden, but may actually energize you. Record your accomplishments and be ready to share them with others to demonstrate your value in the marketplace.

Knowing yourself is the key to managing your career. Invest some time in assessments to understand what really makes you tick. Learn what motivates you, how you prefer to make decisions, what energizes you, and what drains your energy. The more you understand yourself, the more clearly you will also see the people around you and understand their motivations as well.

Always be managing your brand. It is what gets you hired and keeps you there. Be consistent in the way you show yourself to the world. Follow up on what you promise. Know who you are, what you want, and what you stand for, and find clear ways to demonstrate that to those around you. Your brand is the promise that you make to yourself and the world.

Practice putting yourself on paper in ways that resonate with others. Keep track of your accomplishments so that you will have them at hand when you need them. Help others see the skills you have and the benefits they can provide.

Prepare yourself for in-person encounters. Have your personal commercial ready. You never know who you will meet or when. Learn as much as you can about the places that interest you as potential employers. Know the questions that they will ask and have your flexible responses ready. Know what questions YOU want to ask and use them to determine whether an opportunity is a good match for your purpose. Don't forget to say "thank you"!

Remember to utilize your purpose as your yardstick. Will the next opportunity you are considering give you more time or less time to work in your design? Will it ignite your desire? Will it drive your demand? If so, pursue it with all your heart.

EXTRAS AND APPLICATIONS

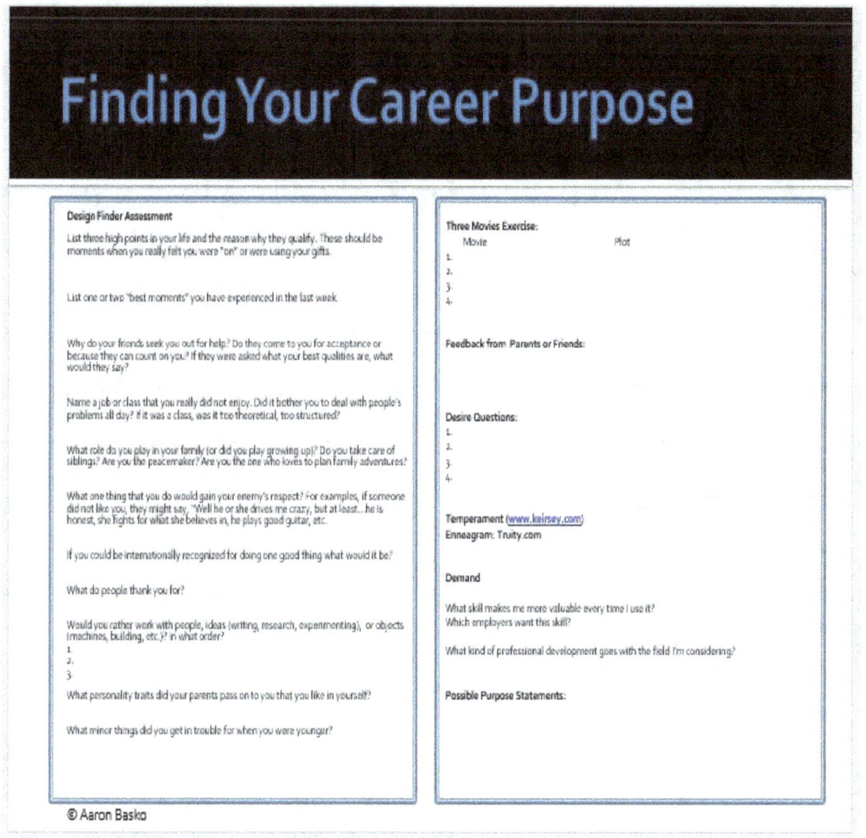

Finding Your Career Purpose

Design Finder Assessment

List three high points in your life and the reason why they qualify. These should be moments when you really felt you were "on" or were using your gifts.

List one or two "best moments" you have experienced in the last week.

Why do your friends seek you out for help? Do they come to you for acceptance or because they can count on you? If they were asked what your best qualities are, what would they say?

Name a job or class that you really did not enjoy. Did it bother you to deal with people's problems all day? If it was a class, was it too theoretical, too structured?

What role do you play in your family (or did you play growing up)? Do you take care of siblings? Are you the peacemaker? Are you the one who loves to plan family adventures?

What one thing that you do would gain your enemy's respect? For examples, if someone did not like you, they might say, "Well he or she drives me crazy, but at least... he is honest, she fights for what she believes in, he plays good guitar, etc.

If you could be internationally recognized for doing one good thing what would it be?

What do people thank you for?

Would you rather work with people, ideas (writing, research, experimenting), or objects (machines, building, etc.)? In what order?
1.
2.
3.

What personality traits did your parents pass on to you that you like in yourself?

What minor things did you get in trouble for when you were younger?

Three Movies Exercise:

Movie	Plot
1.	
2.	
3.	
4.	

Feedback from Parents or Friends:

Desire Questions:
1.
2.
3.
4.

Temperament (www.keirsey.com)
Enneagram: Truity.com

Demand

What skill makes me more valuable every time I use it?
Which employers want this skill?

What kind of professional development goes with the field I'm considering?

Possible Purpose Statements:

© Aaron Basko

Weekly Job Search Log						
	Number	Name	Title	Source	Follow Up	
Contacts						
Informational Interviews	Number	Name	Title	Source	Follow Up	
Referrals/Leads	Number	Name	Title	Source	Follow Up	
Applications	Number	Company	Job Title	Source	Follow Up	Reason

TOP 10 RESUME TIPS

The purpose of a resume is not to get you a job offer, but to interest the employer enough to get you an interview. The best way to achieve this is to:

1. Select an attractive template from the literally hundreds online you can use as a model. Choose something that does not leave too much white space and that divides your information into easily readable sections.

2. Decide whether you want to use an objective statement, (Objective: A position as a sales representative for a major book retailer. — This can be helpful if the job you are applying for is not related to your past experience.), a profile statement (Profile: Successful sales professional with 10 years of experience in retail. — This can be good when the position is clearly connected to your past experience), or no header (good for resumes you will bring to a job fair, etc.).

3. Display your information so that your most important credentials fall in the top one-third of the first page of your resume. The employer's eyes will naturally look here first. Whatever is most relevant or most impressive (work experience, education, training) should appear here.

4. Highlight either the name of the companies you have worked for or the titles you have held. Whichever is more impressive should go first.

5. Use bullets, or even better, small profile paragraphs to give evidence of your success for each position. DO NOT JUST DESCRIBE YOUR JOB DUTIES. Instead, highlight your accomplishments and demonstrate where previous employers trusted you and benefitted from your work with them.

6. Use phrases that begin with powerful action words (managed, built, overhauled, created, analyzed, led, etc.) in place of full sentences.

7. Utilize numbers whenever possible, including number of people served, dollars in sales, satisfaction ratings, percent improvement, years completed, budget amounts, etc.). This makes your writing crisper.

8. If most of your experience is related to the job you want, your job history should be arranged in reverse chronological order (most recent to oldest). If you are trying to change fields, explore whether a functional or combination resume might help (many examples online).

9. Go back and cut out unnecessary information and words that do not really add to the meaning (very, just, only, about, and other words that can be removed from sentences without a substantive change).

10. Proofread, proofread, and proofread again. Now ask someone else (who is a good writer) to proofread it for you. Check the alignment of your dates. Check spelling and grammar. Make sure the tone of the resume sounds like you on your best day. All information should be factual, but you should not be afraid to positively highlight your achievements. That's what a resume is for!

About the Author

 Aaron Basko is an author, speaker, and higher education thought leader with over 25 years of experience in helping people chart a path to their future.

Aaron has served as an enrollment leader at five different colleges and universities, focusing on enrollment growth turnarounds and student success. The author of three career development books focused on career planning (*Help Wanted* and *What's Your Function*), as well as over a dozen articles in *The Chronicle of Higher Education, Inside Higher Ed, University Business, and The Times Higher Education* (U.K.). Aaron has also been quoted four times in *Forbes*, and has served as a consultant for a major U.S. news outlet and multiple colleges and universities. Aaron's passion is to help people see themselves more accurately and to recognize a sense of purpose in their lives.

In 2015, Aaron was selected as a Fulbright Higher Education Administrator grant winner to Japan. He later served on the Fulbright selection panel and as an international student capacity building expert to Fulbright Iceland. He has recruited students and presented internationally in five countries and is a passionate language learner.

In his consulting work, Aaron provides executive coaching and team development. His other books include *The Homeschool College Planner, Master Any Language Faster, and How to Impress U.S. Universities.*